Bucket List Goal

Why we want to do this?

The Experience

Completion Date

Bucket List Goal

Why we want to do this?

The Experience

Completion Date

Bucket List Goal

Why we want to do this?

The Experience

Completion Date

Bucket List Goal

Why we want to do this?

The Experience

Completion Date

Bucket List Goal

Why we want to do this?

The Experience

Completion Date

Bucket List Goal

Why we want to do this?

The Experience

Completion Date

Bucket List Goal

Why We Want to do this?

The Experience

Completion Date

Bucket List Goal

Why we want to do this?

The Experience

Completion Date

& Bucket List Goal &

Why we want to do this?

The Experience

Completion Date

Bucket List Goal

Why we want to do this?

The Experience

Completion Date

Bucket List Goal

Why we want to do this?

The Experience

Completion Date

Bucket List Goal

Why we want to do this?

The Experience

Completion Date

Bucket List Goal

Why We Want to do this?

The Experience

Completion Date

Bucket List Goal

Why we want to do this?

The Experience

Completion Date

Bucket List Goal

Why we want to do this?

The Experience

Completion Date

Bucket List Goal

Why we want to do this?

The Experience

Completion Date

Bucket List Goal

Why we want to do this?

The Experience

Completion Date

Bucket List Goal

Why we want to do this?

The Experience

Completion Date

Bucket List Goal

Why we want to do this?

The Experience

Completion Date

Bucket List Goal

Why we want to do this?

The Experience

Completion Date

Bucket List Goal

Why we want to do this?

The Experience

Completion Date

Bucket List Goal

Why we want to do this?

The Experience

Completion Date

Bucket List Goal

Why we want to do this?

The Experience

Completion Date

Bucket List Goal

Why We Want to do this?

The Experience

Completion Date

Bucket List Goal

Why we want to do this?

The Experience

Completion Date

Bucket List Goal

Why we want to do this?

The Experience

Completion Date

Bucket List Goal

Why we want to do this?

The Experience

Completion Date

Bucket List Goal

Why we want to do this?

The Experience

Completion Date

Bucket List Goal

Why we want to do this?

The Experience

Completion Date

Bucket List Goal

Why We Want to do this?

The Experience

Completion Date

Bucket List Goal

Why we want to do this?

The Experience

Completion Date

Bucket List Goal

Why We Want to do this?

The Experience

Completion Date

Bucket List Goal

Why we want to do this?

The Experience

Completion Date

Bucket List Goal

Why we want to do this?

The Experience

Completion Date

Bucket List Goal

Why we want to do this?

The Experience

Completion Date

Bucket List Goal

Why We Want to do this?

The Experience

Completion Date

Bucket List Goal

_____

Why we want to do this? _____
_____
_____
_____

The Experience

_____
_____
_____
_____
_____
_____
_____
_____
_____
_____
_____
_____
_____
_____
_____
_____
_____
_____

Completion Date _____

Bucket List Goal

Why We Want to do this?

The Experience

Completion Date

Bucket List Goal

Why we want to do this?

The Experience

Completion Date

Bucket List Goal

Why We Want to do this?

The Experience

Completion Date

Bucket List Goal

Why we want to do this?

The Experience

Completion Date

Bucket List Goal

Why We Want to do this?

The Experience

Completion Date

Bucket List Goal

Why we want to do this?

The Experience

Completion Date

Bucket List Goal

Why We Want to do this?

The Experience

Completion Date

Bucket List Goal

Why we want to do this?

The Experience

Completion Date

―――― *Bucket List Goal* ――――

Why we want to do this?

The Experience ――――――――

Completion Date

Bucket List Goal

Why we want to do this?

The Experience

Completion Date

Bucket List Goal

Why we want to do this?

The Experience

Completion Date

Bucket List Goal

Why we want to do this?

The Experience

Completion Date

Bucket List Goal

Why We Want to do this?

The Experience

Completion Date

Bucket List Goal

Why we want to do this?

The Experience

Completion Date

… Bucket List Goal …

Why we want to do this?

The Experience …

Completion Date

Bucket List Goal

Why we want to do this?

The Experience

Completion Date

Bucket List Goal

Why we want to do this?

The Experience

Completion Date

Bucket List Goal

Why We Want to do this?

The Experience

Completion Date

Bucket List Goal

Why We Want to do this?

The Experience

Completion Date

Bucket List Goal

Why we want to do this?

The Experience

Completion Date

Bucket List Goal

Why we want to do this?

The Experience

Completion Date

Bucket List Goal

Why we want to do this?

The Experience

Completion Date

… Bucket List Goal ……

Why we want to do this?

The Experience ……

Completion Date

Bucket List Goal

Why we want to do this?

The Experience

Completion Date

Bucket List Goal

Why we want to do this?

The Experience

Completion Date

Bucket List Goal

Why we want to do this?

The Experience

Completion Date

Bucket List Goal

Why we want to do this?

The Experience

Completion Date

Bucket List Goal

Why we want to do this?

The Experience

Completion Date

Bucket List Goal

Why we want to do this?

The Experience

Completion Date

Bucket List Goal

Why We Want to do this?

The Experience

Completion Date

Bucket List Goal

Why We Want to do this?

The Experience

Completion Date

Bucket List Goal

Why we want to do this?

The Experience

Completion Date

Bucket List Goal

Why We Want to do this?

The Experience

Completion Date

Bucket List Goal

Why We Want to do this?

The Experience

Completion Date

Bucket List Goal

Why We Want to do this?

The Experience

Completion Date

Bucket List Goal

Why We Want to do this?

The Experience

Completion Date

… Bucket List Goal …

Why We Want to do this?

The Experience ——

Completion Date

Bucket List Goal

Why we want to do this?

The Experience

Completion Date

… Bucket List Goal …

Why We Want to do this?

The Experience ———

Completion Date

Bucket List Goal

Why we want to do this?

The Experience

Completion Date

Bucket List Goal

Why We Want to do this?

The Experience

Completion Date

… Bucket List Goal …

Why We Want to do this?

The Experience …

Completion Date

Bucket List Goal

Why We Want to do this?

The Experience

Completion Date

Bucket List Goal

Why we want to do this?

The Experience

Completion Date

Bucket List Goal

Why we want to do this?

The Experience

Completion Date

Bucket List Goal

Why we want to do this?

The Experience

Completion Date

Bucket List Goal

Why we want to do this?

The Experience

Completion Date

Bucket List Goal

Why We Want to Do This?

The Experience

Completion Date

Bucket List Goal

Why We Want to do this?

The Experience

Completion Date

Bucket List Goal

Why we want to do this?

The Experience

Completion Date

Bucket List Goal

Why we want to do this?

The Experience

Completion Date

Bucket List Goal

Why we want to do this?

The Experience

Completion Date

Bucket List Goal

Why we want to do this?

The Experience

Completion Date

Bucket List Goal

Why We Want to do this?

The Experience

Completion Date

… Bucket List Goal ………

Why we want to do this?

The Experience ………

Completion Date

Bucket List Goal

Why we want to do this?

The Experience

Completion Date

Bucket List Goal

Why We Want to do this?

The Experience

Completion Date

Bucket List Goal

Why we want to do this?

The Experience

Completion Date

Bucket List Goal

Why We Want to do this?

The Experience

Completion Date

Bucket List Goal

Why we want to do this?

The Experience

Completion Date

Bucket List Goal

Why we want to do this?

The Experience

Completion Date

Bucket List Goal

Why we want to do this?

The Experience

Completion Date

… Bucket List Goal …

Why we want to do this?

The Experience

Completion Date

Made in the USA
Coppell, TX
21 April 2020